APPLIED AI HANDBOOK

IMPLEMENTING AI WITHOUT BREAKING THE BUSINESS, THE LAW, OR TRUST

DOM JOCUBEIT

REGISTERED OFFICES

Hypermodern Limited Company, 1209 Mountain Road PL NE, STE N, Albuquerque, NM 87110, USA

For details of our global editorial offices, customer services, and more information about Hypermodern products visit us at www.hypermodern.ai.

Hypermodern also publishes its books in a variety of electronic formats and by print-on-demand. Some content that appears in standard print versions of this book may not be available in other formats.

TRADEMARKS

LIMIT OF LIABILITY/DISCLAIMER OF WARRANTY

CONTENTS

AUDIENCE AND SCOPE

HOW TO USE THIS BOOK

This handbook is written for **AI practitioners who are directly involved in implementing systems inside real organizations,** people who are accountable for outcomes, even when they do not control every decision.

It is designed to be used as a **decision guide**, not as a reference manual or a compliance artifact. Its value lies in how it constrains thinking, surfaces tradeoffs, and supports judgment at moments where momentum would otherwise replace deliberation.

WHO THIS BOOK IS FOR

This book is for readers who:

- Are responsible for translating AI capability into operational systems
- Participate in or influence decisions about scope, design, deployment, or continuation

- Must balance technical possibility with organizational, legal, and ethical constraint
- Need language to pause, challenge, or stop initiatives, not just advance them

If you are expected to answer for how a system behaves after deployment, this book is written for you.

WHO THIS BOOK IS NOT FOR

This book is **not**:

- A technical guide to building or training models
- A catalog of tools, vendors, or architectures
- A compliance checklist or regulatory framework
- A substitute for legal advice or executive authority
- A general introduction to artificial intelligence

It does not attempt to persuade organizations *to* adopt AI, nor does it argue that AI adoption is inevitable.

HOW THIS BOOK SHOULD NOT BE USED

This handbook should not be used:

- As a symbolic artifact to signal responsibility without changing decisions
- As a post-hoc justification for systems already deployed
- As a way to transfer accountability without authority
- As a means to bypass legal, regulatory, or human review

If the book is cited without engaging its decision gates, it is being misused.

WHAT THIS BOOK PROVIDES

This book provides:

- A lifecycle-oriented way to think about AI implementation
- Explicit decision points where stopping or pausing is valid
- Language for making risk, cost, and responsibility visible
- A framework for treating restraint as competence

It assumes good faith, professional judgment, and a willingness to accept uncomfortable conclusions.

RELATIONSHIP TO COMPANION ARTIFACTS

The companion artifacts associated with this book are **working documents**, not forms to be submitted or completed for compliance.

They are intended to be adapted, debated, and revised within the context of real organizational decision-making.

Completing an artifact does not confer approval. Decisions do.

SCOPE

This book focuses on **implementation**.

It begins before design, continues through deployment, and ends after systems are retired. It does not prescribe what goals organizations should pursue, only how to responsibly build, operate, and end systems once those goals are proposed.

Responsibility, in this context, is not a moral stance. It is an operational practice.

LETTER TO THE READER

If you are reading this, you are probably responsible for turning "AI" from an idea into a system that actually operates inside a real organization.

Not a demo.

Not a research artifact.

Not a slide deck.

A system that touches data it did not generate, influences decisions it does not fully own, and operates under constraints that are only partially articulated.

This book is written for you.

It assumes you already know that AI is powerful. It assumes you already understand the basics of models, data pipelines, and deployment. It does not try to convince you that AI matters, nor does it promise that it will be easy, fast, or transformative by default.

Instead, it starts from a more uncomfortable premise:

Most AI systems fail not because the models are weak, but because the implementation ignores the institutional reality they are embedded in.

They fail quietly, by being unused, mistrusted, or worked around.

They fail loudly, by creating legal exposure, ethical breaches, or reputational damage.

And sometimes they "succeed" technically while still degrading trust, accountability, or organizational clarity.

If you have ever been asked to "just ship something" while also being told to "make it compliant," "prove ROI," and "use AI responsibly," you already know the gap this book is trying to address.

WHAT THIS BOOK IS (AND IS NOT)

This is not a book about algorithms.

It is a book about **decisions**.

Specifically:

- decisions made under uncertainty,
- decisions made without full authority,
- decisions whose consequences often surface months after deployment,
- and decisions for which you may be held accountable even if you did not set the incentives.

This handbook treats AI systems as **socio-technical systems**, composed not just of models and data, but of people, processes, power structures, regulations, and economic realities.

Governance, compliance, ethics, cost, user experience, and organizational buy-in are not presented as separate topics to be "handled" later. They are treated as **design constraints** that shape what is technically viable from the start.

If you are looking for best practices in isolation, this is not that book.

If you are looking for a maturity model to benchmark yourself against peers, this is not that book.

If you are looking for a narrative about the future of AI, this is not that book.

This is a field manual for implementation.

THE READER THIS BOOK ASSUMES

This book assumes you are competent.

It assumes you are already making tradeoffs, whether or not they have been made explicit. It assumes you understand that every architecture choice embeds risk, that every vendor contract has second-order effects, and that every metric shapes behavior downstream.

It also assumes something else, less often acknowledged:

That you are operating in an environment where responsibility often exceeds authority.

You may not control the legal interpretation.

You may not control executive expectations.

You may not control timelines or budgets.

But you will still be expected to explain why a system behaved the way it did, and why it was built that way in the first place.

This book is written to help you make those explanations coherent, defensible, and grounded in reality.

HOW TO USE THIS HANDBOOK

This book is organized around the **lifecycle of an AI implementation**, not around abstract topics.

You can read it end to end, but it is also designed to be used:

- before green-lighting a project,
- during a design review,
- ahead of a deployment decision,
- or when deciding whether to shut a system down.

Throughout the book, you will find:

- common failure modes that are rarely documented,
- tensions that cannot be resolved, only managed,
- and guidance that sometimes concludes the correct decision is *not* to build.

That is intentional.

A system you choose not to deploy is often the most responsible outcome.

A FINAL NOTE

AI implementation is increasingly treated as a technical problem with a moral appendix or a legal checklist. That framing is inadequate.

In practice, you are building infrastructure that redistributes agency, reshapes accountability, and encodes assumptions about how decisions should be made.

This book does not offer certainty. It offers **orientation**.

If it helps you:

- surface hidden risks earlier,
- articulate tradeoffs more clearly,
- resist pressure to oversimplify,
- or decide not to deploy a system that should not exist,

then it has done its job.

Everything that follows is written in that spirit.

USING THE COMPANION ARTIFACTS

This book is accompanied by a set of **living artifacts** designed to support real decisions in real organizational contexts.

They are not templates to be completed for compliance, nor checklists to be satisfied once and forgotten. They are working documents intended to be used, challenged, revised, and revisited over time.

WHAT THE COMPANION ARTIFACTS ARE

The companion artifacts are a small set of decision memos that align with the lifecycle described in this book. Each artifact corresponds to a specific decision gate:

- whether a system should exist,
- whether its risks are acceptable,
- what design commitments are being made,
- how the system will be integrated and governed in practice,
- and whether it should continue to operate or be retired.

Their purpose is to make responsibility visible at moments where momentum would otherwise substitute for judgment.

WHAT THE COMPANION ARTIFACTS ARE NOT

The artifacts are **not**:

- approval forms or authorization mechanisms,
- substitutes for legal, regulatory, or executive review,
- documentation exercises performed after decisions are made,
- or guarantees of responsible outcomes.

Completing an artifact does not confer legitimacy, feasibility, or approval. Decisions do.

HOW TO USE THE ARTIFACTS

The artifacts are most effective when:

- drafted early, before commitments harden,
- completed collaboratively across roles,
- treated as provisional rather than final,
- and revisited when context, scope, or behavior changes.

They may be copied, adapted, or integrated into existing organizational processes. Fidelity to intent matters more than fidelity to format.

LIVING DOCUMENTS

Each artifact is deliberately incomplete.

They are designed to surface uncertainty, disagreement, and tradeoffs, not to resolve them automatically. As systems evolve, the artifacts should evolve with them, creating a record of how decisions were made and revisited over time.

If an artifact becomes static, it has likely stopped serving its purpose.

RELATIONSHIP TO THIS BOOK

This book provides orientation and structure. The companion artifacts provide working surfaces.

Used together, they help practitioners slow down when it matters, document responsibility without diffusing it, and treat restraint as a form of competence.

Used separately, neither is sufficient.

ACCESS AND ADAPTATION

The companion artifacts are provided as editable documents intended for practical use. They may be adapted to fit organizational context, governance structures, or regulatory environments.

No artifact should be treated as universally applicable without judgment.

The responsibility for how these artifacts are used remains with the practitioner.

ACCESSING THE COMPANION ARTIFACTS

To get access to the companion artifacts, please visit the Hypermodern website:

https://hypermodern.ai/publications/applied-ai-handbook

CHAPTER 1
PROBLEM FRAMING AND LEGITIMACY

Before architecture, before data pipelines, before vendor selection, there is a more fundamental question that determines the fate of every AI system:

Should this system exist at all?

This is not a philosophical exercise. It is an implementation decision with concrete consequences. Systems that are poorly framed at inception tend to accumulate technical debt, governance risk, and organizational resistance regardless of how sophisticated the underlying models may be.

This chapter focuses on establishing *legitimacy*, the conditions under which an AI system is justified, defensible, and viable inside a real institution. Without legitimacy, implementation effort merely accelerates failure.

THE COST OF STARTING TOO SOON

Organizations rarely fail to imagine AI use cases. They fail by committing to solutions before agreeing on the problem.

Common symptoms of premature commitment include:

- A mandate to "use AI" without a clearly articulated failure being addressed
- Success metrics defined in terms of model performance rather than organizational outcomes
- An implicit assumption that automation is inherently beneficial
- A demo-driven sense of progress disconnected from operational reality

Once a technical path is chosen, it becomes increasingly difficult to revisit first principles. Architecture choices harden assumptions. Data pipelines encode scope. Vendor contracts lock in dependencies. Governance is retrofitted rather than designed.

Problem framing is therefore not a preliminary step, it is a control point.

LEGITIMACY AS A GATE

A use case describes *what* a system might do. Legitimacy determines *whether it should proceed.*

At minimum, legitimacy requires four conditions: a real problem, a justified use of AI, a named outcome owner, and explicit stop conditions.

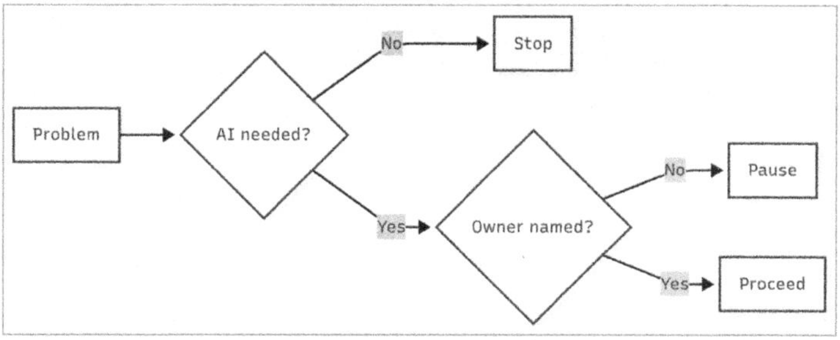

Figure 1.1 - Legitimacy is a gate, not a gradient. Systems either meet the bar or they do not.

Failure to meet any one of these conditions should pause implementation. Legitimacy is not granted by enthusiasm, executive sponsorship, or technological novelty. It is granted by alignment between problem, method, and institutional responsibility.

PROBLEM DEFINITION IS GOVERNANCE

Problem framing is often treated as a product or engineering exercise. In practice, it is an act of governance.

How a problem is defined determines:

- Which data may be used
- Which populations are affected
- Which errors are tolerable
- Which decisions are delegated to machines
- Which risks are normalized

These choices embed values into system behavior long before any model is trained. Treat early framing decisions as effectively irreversible unless proven otherwise.

THE NON-AI COUNTERFACTUAL

Every proposed AI system should be evaluated against a serious non-AI alternative.

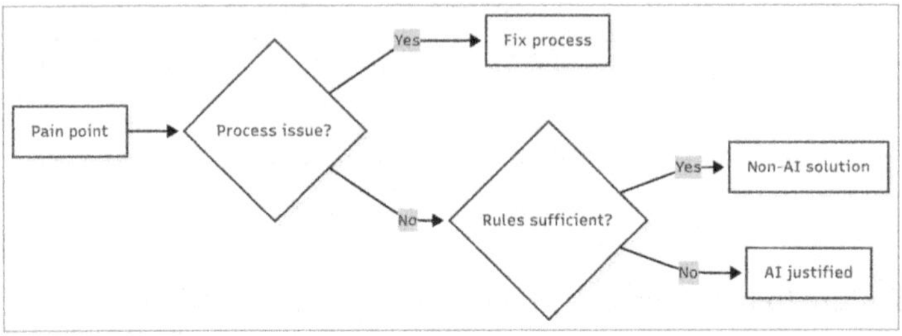

Figure 1.2 - If the value disappears without AI, the problem was misframed.

If the AI advantage collapses under this comparison, AI is being used as a proxy for organizational change rather than as a justified tool. Choosing not to build is often the most responsible outcome of rigorous framing.

OWNERSHIP AND THE ACCOUNTABILITY TEST

One of the most consistent failure patterns in AI implementation is the separation of authority from accountability.

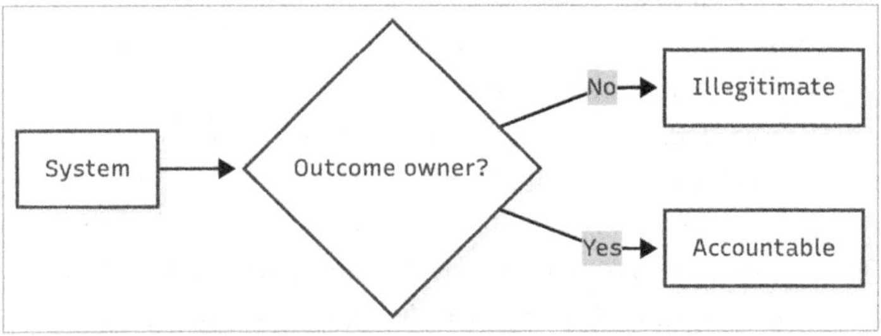

Figure 1.3 - Responsibility without ownership produces risk; ownership without authority produces failure.

Before proceeding, it must be explicit who owns outcomes, who can change scope, and who can stop the system. Ownership is not a role; it is a commitment backed by decision rights.

LEGITIMACY OVER TIME

Legitimacy is not permanent. Systems drift as data, incentives, and policies change.

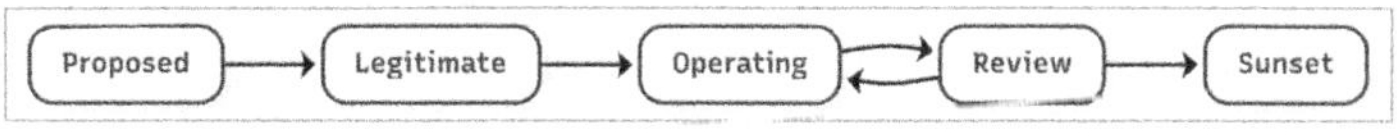

Figure 1.4 - Review is normal. Sunsetting is a valid outcome.

A legitimate system is one that remains defensible over time, not just at launch. If you cannot explain why the system should continue to exist as conditions change, you are not ready to deploy it.

FRAMING CHECKLIST

Before moving to design, you should be able to answer, concisely and in writing:

- What problem are we solving, and for whom?
- Why is AI the appropriate mechanism?
- Who owns the system's outcomes?
- What harms are plausible, and who bears them?
- Under what conditions would we stop?

If these answers are vague, contested, or politically inconvenient, that is a signal, not an obstacle.

CLOSING

Legitimacy is the foundation of every downstream decision. Without it, feasibility analysis becomes risk laundering and implementation becomes liability accumulation.

The next chapter moves from legitimacy to **feasibility**, examining how data realities, risk surfaces, and institutional constraints determine what can actually be built, even when a system is justified in principle.

CHAPTER 2
FEASIBILITY AND THE RISK SURFACE

Legitimacy answers whether a system *should* exist. Feasibility determines whether it *can* exist in practice, given data realities, institutional constraints, and the risks an organization is actually capable of absorbing.

Many AI initiatives fail in this transition. A system may be justified in principle and still be infeasible in context. Treating feasibility as a purely technical question is the fastest way to discover this too late.

This chapter reframes feasibility as an assessment of the **risk surface**: the full set of technical, legal, operational, and reputational exposures created by implementing the system.

FEASIBILITY IS NOT TECHNICAL VIABILITY

A model that can be trained is not necessarily a system that can be operated.

Technical viability answers narrow questions:

- Can we acquire data?
- Can we train a model?

- Can we deploy it?

Feasibility asks harder ones:

- Can we *legally* use the data we have?
- Can we explain or audit outcomes when required?
- Can the organization respond when the system is wrong?
- Can the system survive scrutiny beyond its launch window?

If feasibility is assessed only by engineering readiness, risk is merely displaced downstream.

MAPPING THE RISK SURFACE

Every AI system creates a risk surface that extends beyond its immediate function.

At a minimum, feasibility requires exposure across five domains to be identified and owned:

- **Data risk** — provenance, consent, quality, and drift
- **Model risk** — error modes, brittleness, and misuse
- **Operational risk** — integration into workflows and failure handling
- **Legal and regulatory risk** — compliance, auditability, liability
- **Reputational risk** — trust, perception, and external scrutiny

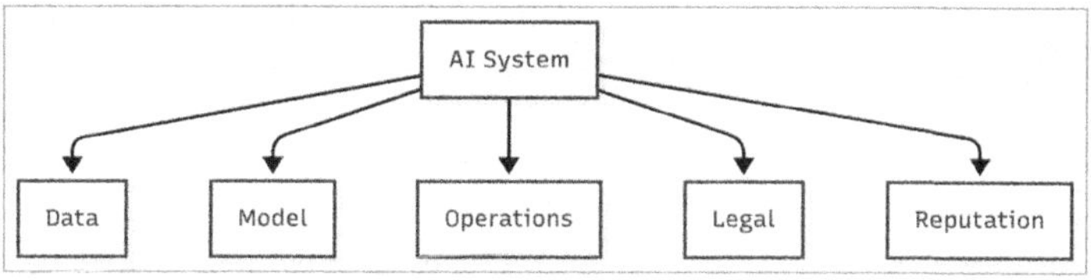

Figure 2.1 - Feasibility requires understanding the full risk surface, not just the model.

Ignoring a domain does not eliminate the risk; it merely removes it from conscious design.

DATA REALITY CHECK

Data feasibility is the most common source of hidden failure.

Before design proceeds, the following must be true:

- Data sources are lawful, consented, and documented
- Data meaning is stable enough to support the task
- Systemic gaps, bias, and noise are understood
- Data ownership and retention obligations are clear

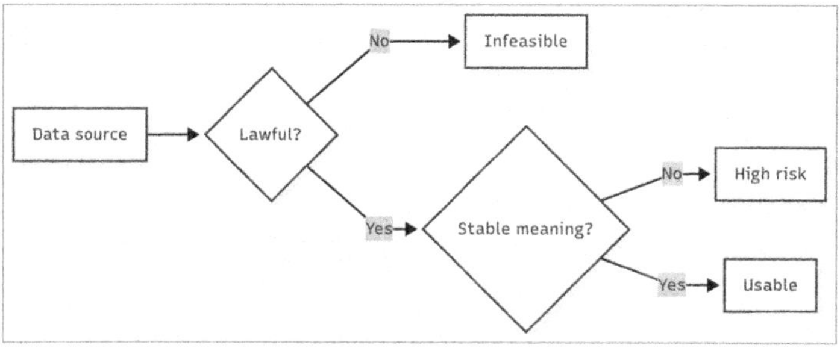

Figure 2.2 - Data that cannot be defended cannot support a system.

If data legality or meaning is ambiguous, feasibility is provisional at best. No model choice can compensate for this.

OPERATIONAL FEASIBILITY

An AI system is feasible only if the organization can *operate* it.

Operational feasibility requires:

- Clear integration into human workflows
- Defined escalation and override paths
- Monitoring and incident response
- Maintenance ownership over time

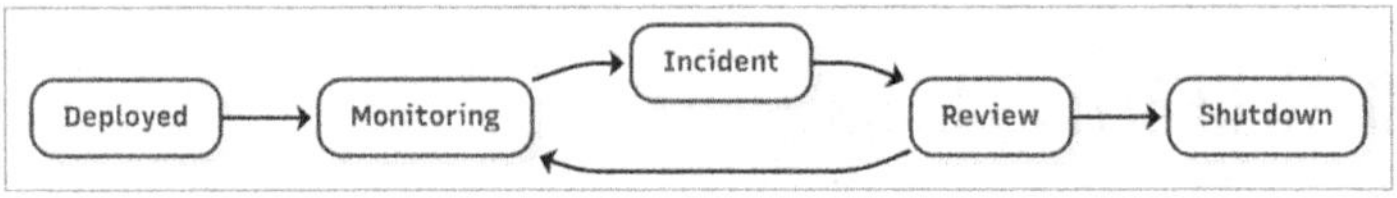

Figure 2.3 - Operations determine whether risk is contained or amplified.

If no one is responsible for monitoring, no one will notice failure until it becomes public.

LEGAL AND REGULATORY CONSTRAINTS

Legal feasibility is often discovered reactively. This is a mistake.

Before deployment, confirm:

- Applicable regulatory regimes
- Documentation and audit requirements
- Explainability and record-keeping obligations
- Liability allocation across vendors and teams

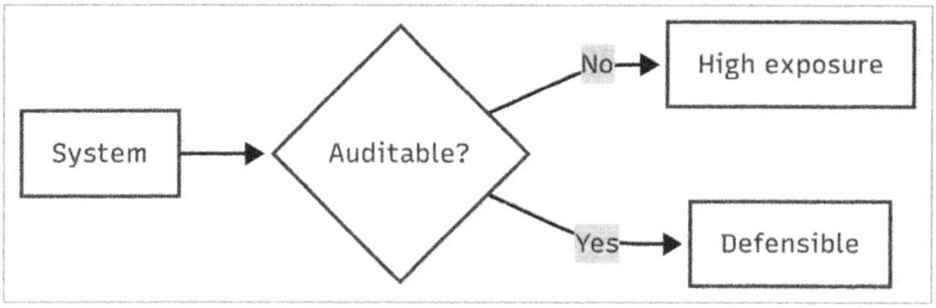

Figure 2.5 - If you cannot explain or reconstruct behavior, you cannot defend it.

When legal feasibility is unclear, the default assumption should be constraint, not permissiveness.

REPUTATIONAL LOAD

Some systems are technically and legally feasible but fragile by reputation.

Assess:

- Public visibility of the system
- Sensitivity of the domain
- Asymmetry between benefit and potential harm

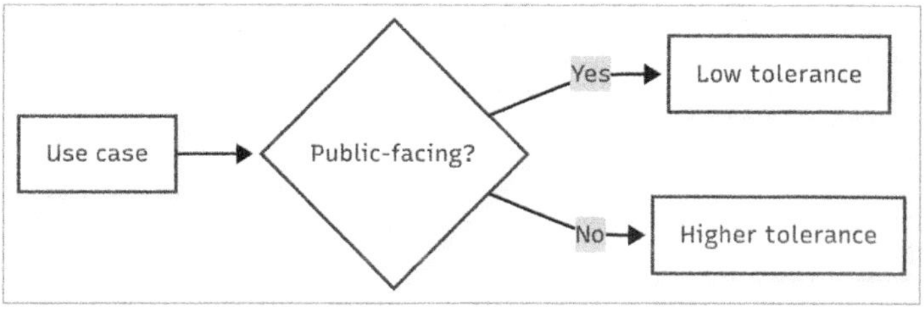

Figure 2.6 - Reputational risk compresses error budgets.

A small technical error can become an existential problem when public trust is at stake.

FEASIBILITY AS A DECISION

Feasibility is not a property of the system. It is a decision by the organization to accept a specific risk profile.

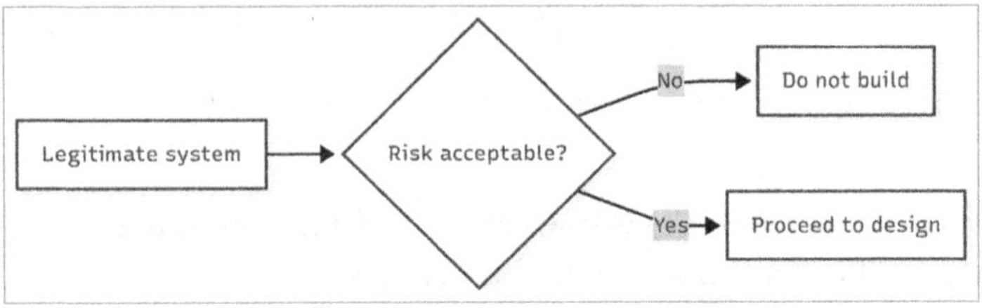

Figure 2.7 - Proceeding is an explicit acceptance of risk, not a default.

If risk acceptance cannot be made explicit and owned, the system is not feasible, regardless of technical promise.

CLOSING

A feasible AI system is one whose risks are visible, bounded, and owned. When feasibility is treated as optimism, implementation becomes an exercise in deferred accountability.

The next chapter moves from feasibility to **system design**, examining how architectural choices encode governance, cost, and control long before deployment.

CHAPTER 3
SYSTEM DESIGN AS GOVERNANCE

Once a system is legitimate and feasible, attention typically turns to architecture. This is often framed as a technical phase: selecting models, choosing vendors, defining interfaces.

That framing is incomplete.

System design is governance by other means. Architectural decisions encode authority, accountability, cost, and control long before any policy document is written. By the time formal governance is discussed, most of the consequential choices have already been made.

This chapter examines system design not as optimization, but as institutional commitment.

ARCHITECTURE AS A COMMITMENT

Every architectural choice constrains future options.

Decisions about centralization vs distribution, coupling vs modularity, and automation vs support determine:

- Who can intervene when things go wrong

- What can be audited or explained
- How expensive change will be
- Where power and responsibility reside

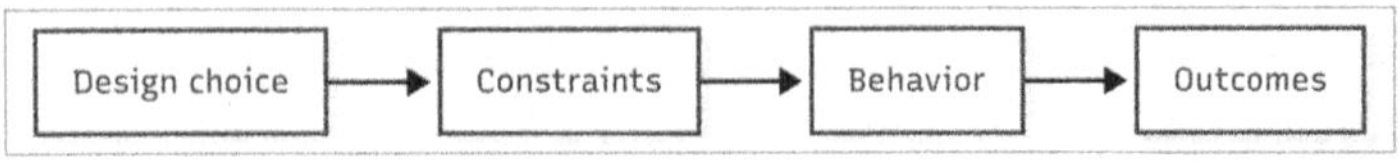

Figure 3.1 - Architecture determines behavior before policy intervenes.

Design should therefore be treated as an irreversible act unless proven otherwise.

BUILD, BUY, OR DELEGATE

One of the earliest design decisions is whether to build internally, buy from a vendor, or delegate capability to a platform.

Each option carries a distinct governance profile.

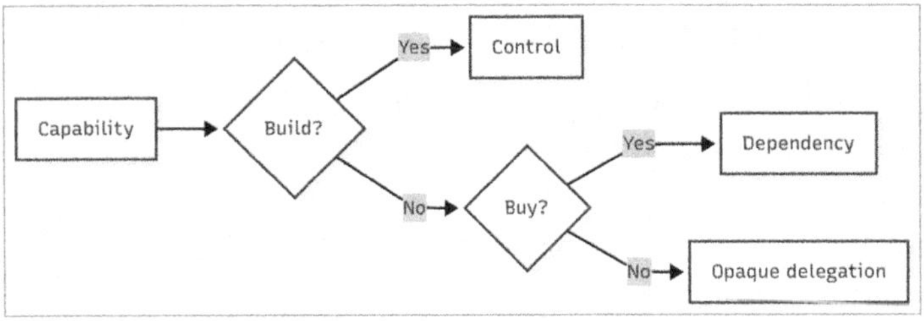

Figure 3.2 - Convenience trades directly against control.

Building increases responsibility and cost but preserves agency. Buying accelerates delivery but externalizes risk. Delegation maximizes speed at the expense of visibility and leverage.

No option is neutral. Treat this as a governance choice, not a procurement one.

MODEL CLASS AND ERROR SHAPE

Different model classes fail differently. Feasibility established *whether* error is acceptable; design determines *how* error manifests.

Key considerations include:

- Predictable vs emergent error patterns
- Sensitivity to distribution shift
- Ability to constrain or bound outputs

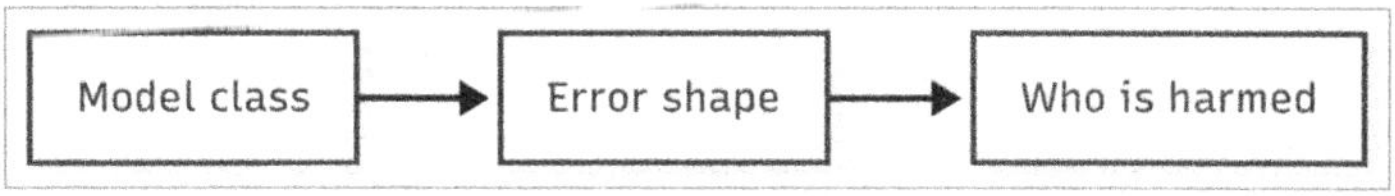

Figure 3.3 - Error is not abstract; it is distributed.

Selecting a model class is therefore an ethical and operational decision, not merely a performance one.

HUMAN-IN-THE-LOOP IS A DESIGN CHOICE

Human oversight is often discussed as a safeguard. In practice, it is an architectural decision that redistributes labor, authority, and blame.

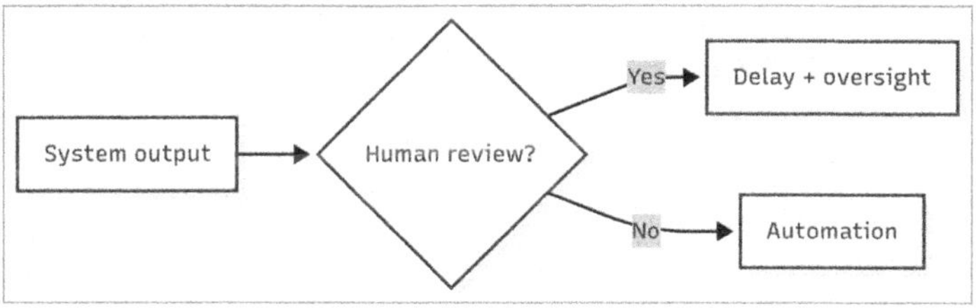

Figure 3.4 - Oversight shifts responsibility; it does not eliminate risk.

Poorly designed human-in-the-loop systems create false

assurance, overload reviewers, and concentrate liability without authority.

Design human involvement deliberately, or do not include it at all.

INTERFACES, NOT MODELS, SHAPE EXPERIENCE

End users rarely experience a model directly. They experience interfaces, defaults, and failure modes.

Design choices about:

- How outputs are presented
- Whether uncertainty is visible
- What actions are easy or hard

will determine trust and adoption more than model accuracy.

Figure 3.5 - Interfaces operationalize values.

Interface design is therefore a first-order governance concern.

COST SURFACES AND LOCK-IN

Cost is not limited to compute.

Design decisions determine:

- Ongoing operational expense
- Switching costs
- Dependency on proprietary formats or APIs
- Ability to exit or renegotiate

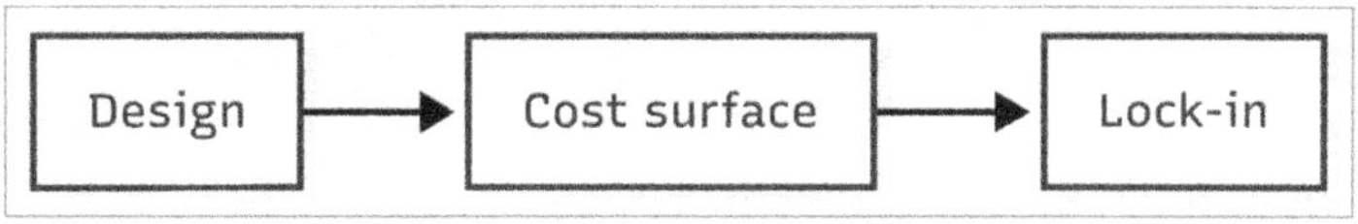

Figure 3.6 - Cheap to launch does not mean cheap to own.

If exit costs are undefined, the organization has already committed more than it realizes.

DESIGNING FOR INTERVENTION

A governable system is one that can be intervened upon.

Intervention requires:

- Observable state
- Adjustable parameters
- Clear escalation paths

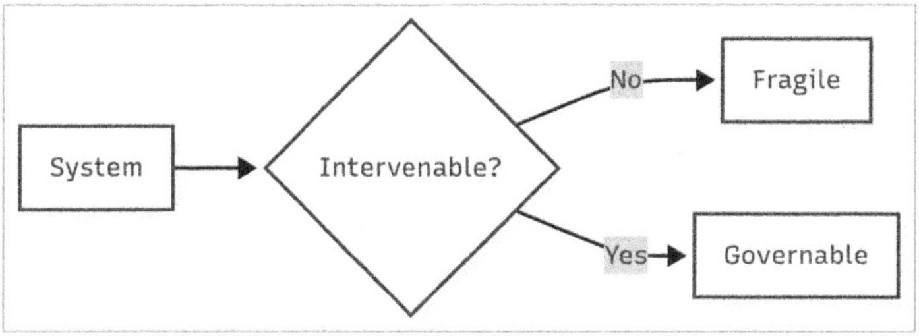

Figure 3.7 - If you cannot intervene, you do not control the system.

Systems designed only for steady-state performance fail catastrophically under stress.

CLOSING

System design determines who bears risk, who holds power, and who is accountable long before deployment.

Treating architecture as a neutral technical exercise is a category error. Design is where governance either becomes operational, or becomes impossible.

The next chapter turns to **organizational integration**, examining how incentives, workflows, and culture determine whether a well-designed system survives contact with reality.

CHAPTER 4
ORGANIZATIONAL INTEGRATION

A system that is legitimate, feasible, and well designed can still fail, quietly and completely, once it encounters an organization.

Most AI systems do not fail because they are rejected outright. They fail because they are *worked around*, ignored, selectively used, or blamed when convenient. These failures are rarely technical. They are organizational.

This chapter examines what happens after design, when an AI system must coexist with incentives, workflows, power structures, and human judgment. Integration is not adoption; it is alignment.

INTEGRATION IS NOT DEPLOYMENT

Deployment is a technical event. Integration is a behavioral outcome.

A system is integrated only when:

- People understand when to use it and when not to

- Its outputs are trusted appropriately—not blindly or dismissively
- Responsibility for outcomes is socially clear

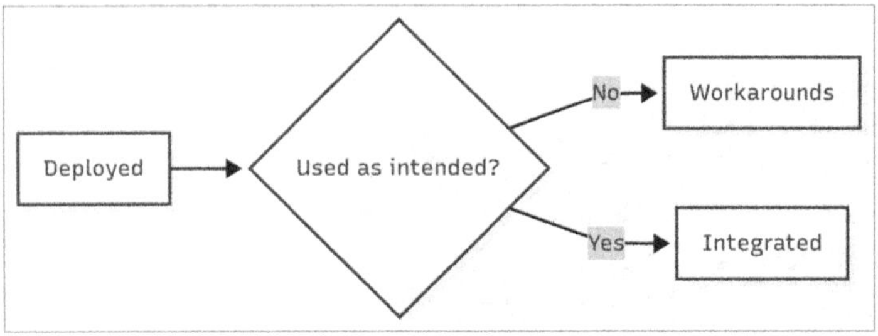

Figure 4.1 - Deployed systems fail quietly when integration is assumed.

Deployed systems fail quietly when integration is assumed.

INCENTIVES SHAPE REALITY

Organizations behave according to incentives, not policies.

If incentives reward speed, volume, or short-term metrics, AI systems will be used to optimize for those outcomes, regardless of stated principles.

Common misalignments include:

- Systems that improve quality but slow throughput
- Systems that surface uncertainty in cultures that punish hesitation
- Systems that require judgment in environments optimized for compliance

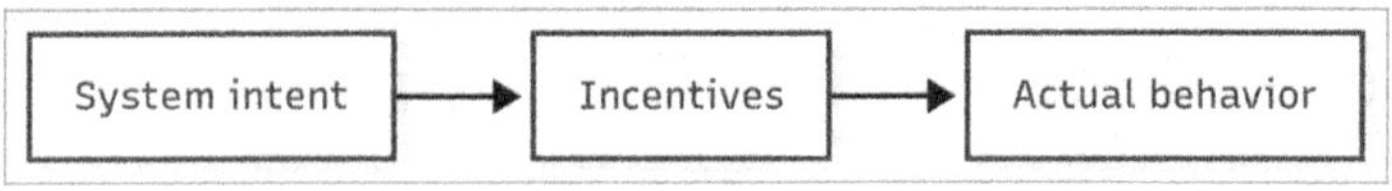

Figure 4.2 - Incentives determine how systems are actually used.

Until incentives are aligned, training and communication will have limited effect.

TRUST CALIBRATION

Trust is neither binary nor static. Users must learn *how much* to trust a system and *when* to rely on it.

Over-trust leads to automation bias. Under-trust leads to abandonment.

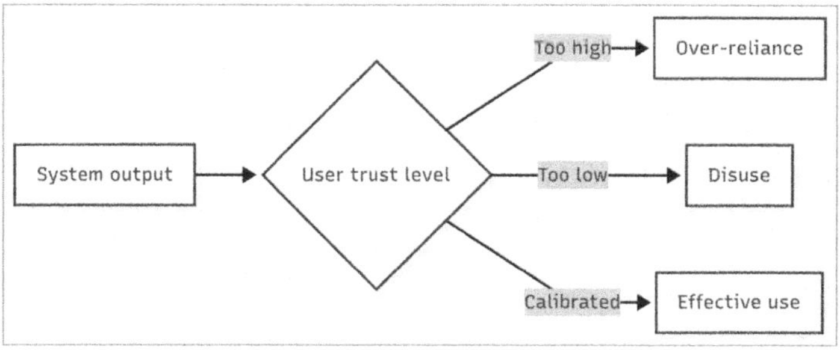

Figure 4.3 - Both over-trust and under-trust are integration failures.

Trust calibration depends on transparency, feedback, and consistent behavior, not on exhortation.

WORKFLOW FIT

AI systems do not replace workflows; they insert themselves into them.

Poor workflow fit manifests as:

- Additional steps added to already constrained processes
- Context switching at high-cognitive-load moments
- Outputs arriving too early or too late to be actionable

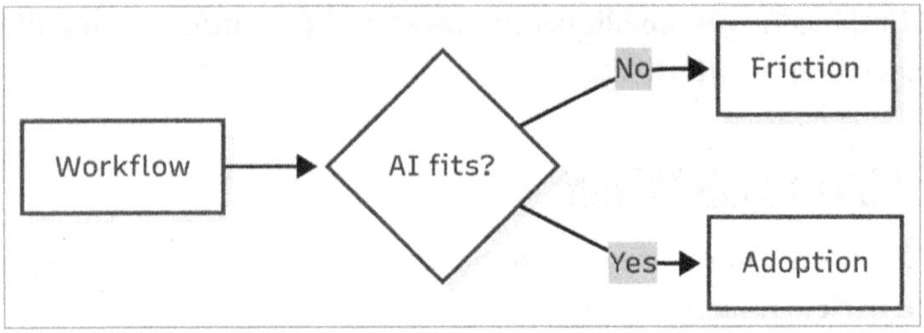

Figure 4.4 - Friction is often misdiagnosed as resistance.

When users resist a system, the problem is often design timing, not attitude.

AUTHORITY, OVERRIDES, AND BLAME

Integration fails when authority is ambiguous.

Users must know:

- When they are allowed to override the system
- When they are expected to defer
- Who is accountable for outcomes

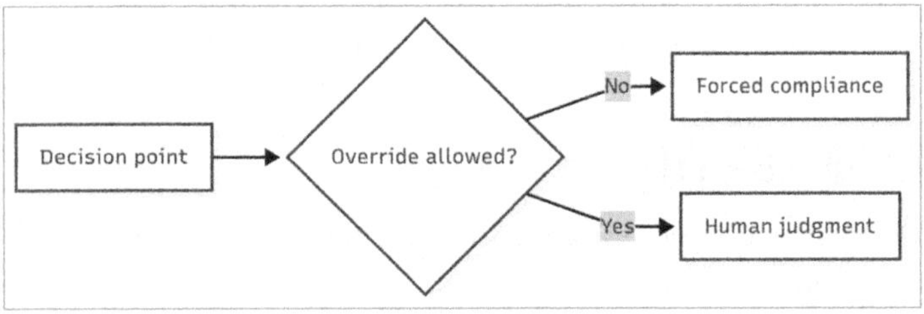

Figure 4.5 - Ambiguous authority concentrates blame without power.

Systems that remove discretion without removing accountability create moral and legal risk.

TRAINING AS SENSE-MAKING

Training is often treated as knowledge transfer. For AI systems, it is sense-making.

Effective training explains:

- What the system is good at
- Where it fails
- What signals to watch for
- How to escalate concerns

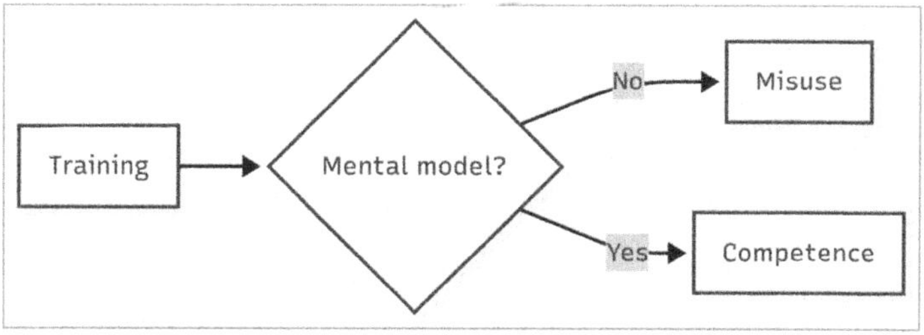

Figure 4.6 - Without a shared mental model, training is performative.

The goal is not compliance, but informed judgment.

MEASURING USE, NOT JUST PERFORMANCE

Integration must be measured.

Beyond model metrics, track:

- Adoption and abandonment rates
- Override frequency and patterns
- Time-to-decision impacts
- Incident reports and near-misses

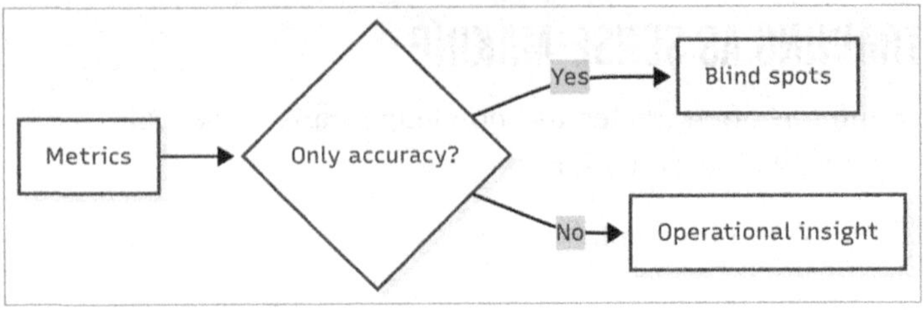

Figure 4.7 - What you measure determines what you notice.

If integration is not observed, it cannot be improved.

CLOSING

Organizational integration is where responsibility becomes real. It is where abstract commitments to ethics, governance, and value are tested against everyday behavior.

A system that cannot be integrated safely and coherently should not be deployed, regardless of its technical merit.

The next chapter turns to **economics and measurement**, examining how cost, ROI, and accounting choices shape which systems persist, and which quietly become liabilities.

CHAPTER 5
ECONOMICS, ROI, AND COST ACCOUNTING

AI systems are often justified with economic language, efficiency, scale, return on investment. Yet few AI initiatives are evaluated with economic rigor once they move beyond approval.

This gap produces two pathologies: systems that are declared successful because they exist, and systems that persist long after their economic justification has evaporated.

This chapter treats economics not as a business case artifact, but as an **operational discipline**. Value must be measurable, costs must be visible, and continuation must be a choice.

ROI IS NOT A NUMBER

ROI is frequently reduced to a single figure produced during project approval. In practice, ROI is a hypothesis that must survive contact with reality.

Common failures include:

- Benefits counted once, costs counted continuously
- Labor savings assumed but never realized

- Revenue attribution disconnected from actual use
- Risk externalities excluded entirely

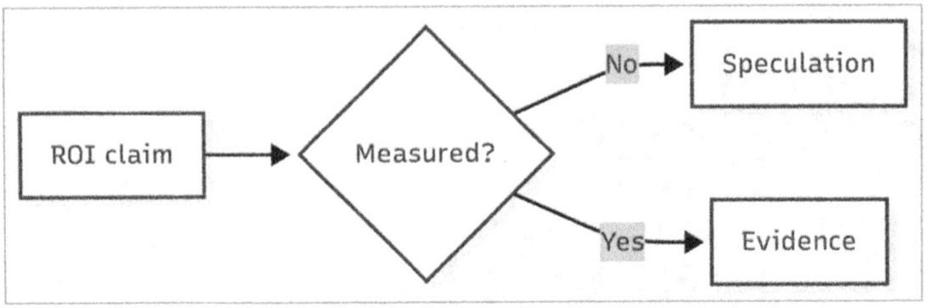

Figure 5.1 - Unmeasured ROI is narrative, not analysis.

Treat ROI as something to be *tested,* not asserted.

DEFINING VALUE IN OPERATIONAL TERMS

Before measurement, value must be defined in ways that survive scrutiny.

Operational value typically falls into one or more categories:

- Time saved per decision
- Error reduction in high-cost processes
- Throughput improvement without quality loss
- Risk avoided or exposure reduced

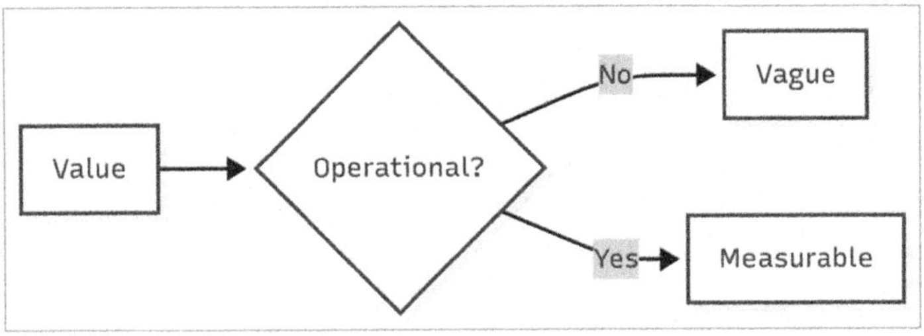

Figure 5.2 - If value cannot be observed in operations, it cannot be defended.

If value cannot be observed in operations, it cannot be defended.

THE FULL COST SURFACE

Compute costs are visible. Most other costs are not.

A realistic cost model includes:

- Data acquisition, cleaning, and governance
- Model development and evaluation
- Integration and workflow redesign
- Monitoring, incident response, and retraining
- Legal, compliance, and audit overhead
- Training, change management, and support

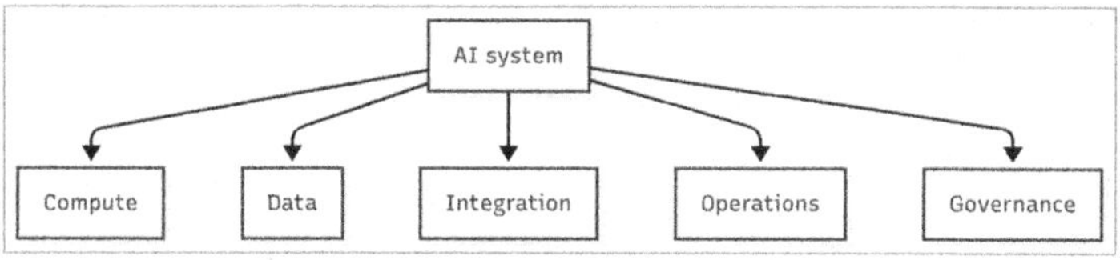

Figure 5.3 - Compute is rarely the dominant cost over time.

Ignoring non-compute costs leads to systematic underestimation.

FIXED, VARIABLE, AND HIDDEN COSTS

AI systems blur traditional cost categories.

- **Fixed costs** appear variable due to usage-based pricing
- **Variable costs** spike unpredictably under load or drift
- **Hidden costs** emerge only during failure or audit

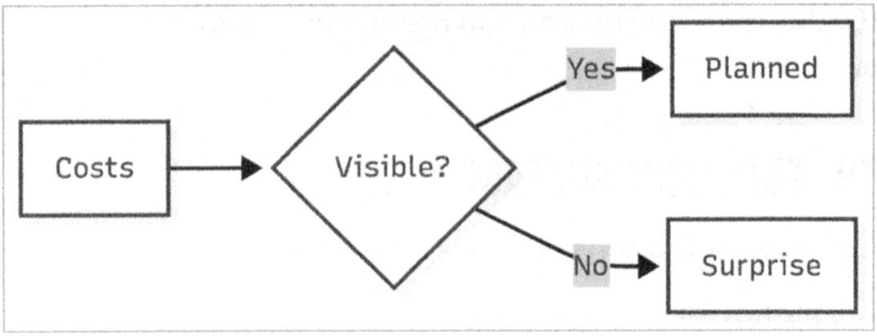

Figure 5.4 - Hidden costs surface under stress, not during planning.

Feasible systems account for stress scenarios, not just steady state.

COST, QUALITY, AND TRUST TRADEOFFS

Economic pressure shapes system behavior.

When costs rise, organizations respond by:

- Reducing human oversight
- Increasing automation thresholds
- Narrowing monitoring

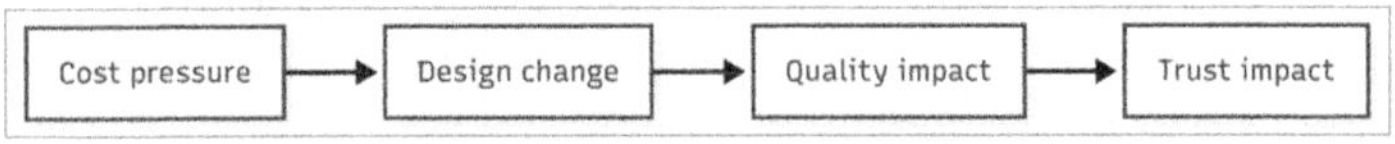

Figure 5.5 - Cost optimization often degrades trust indirectly.

Short-term savings can create long-term liabilities.

MEASURING WHAT PERSISTS

Systems persist not because they are valuable, but because they are funded.

Measurement must therefore support **continuation decisions**:

- Is value increasing, stable, or declining?
- Are costs predictable or drifting?
- Are risks accumulating faster than benefits?

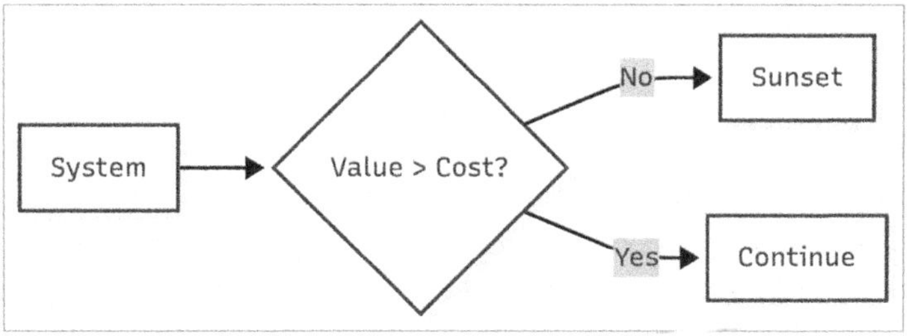

Figure 5.6 - Continuation is an economic decision, not a technical one.

Without explicit continuation gates, systems default to permanence.

WHEN TO STOP

Stopping an AI system is often framed as failure. Economically, it is often success.

Signals that justify stopping include:

- Marginal value approaching zero
- Rising operational or compliance burden
- Degradation of trust or reputation

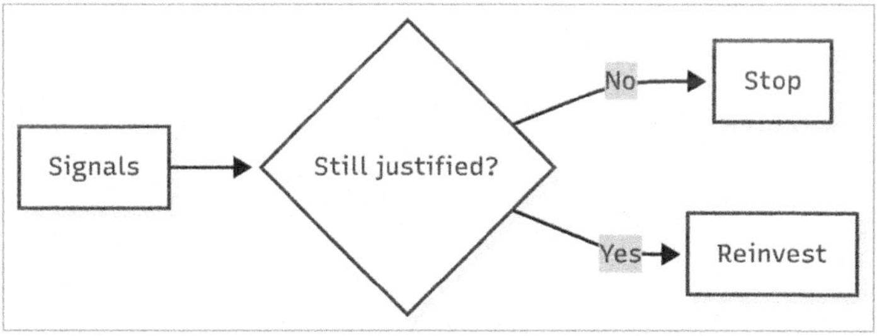

Figure 5.7 - Sunsetting is a form of discipline.

Organizations that cannot stop systems accumulate economic and ethical debt.

CLOSING

Economic discipline is what prevents AI systems from becoming permanent experiments.

Clear cost accounting, defensible ROI measurement, and explicit continuation decisions are not constraints on innovation, they are what allow innovation to persist responsibly.

The next chapter turns to **governance, compliance, and ethics**, examining how formal oversight interacts with the systems already in operation.

CHAPTER 6
GOVERNANCE, COMPLIANCE, AND ETHICS IN PRACTICE

Governance, compliance, and ethics are often treated as external constraints on AI systems, rules to satisfy after design, implementation, and deployment.

In practice, they are *properties of the system as built*.

Policies do not govern systems. Systems govern behavior. Formal oversight matters, but it is effective only insofar as it aligns with how systems actually operate.

This chapter reframes governance, compliance, and ethics as **operational disciplines**, embedded throughout the lifecycle rather than appended to it.

GOVERNANCE IS NOT DOCUMENTATION

Many organizations equate governance with artifacts: principles, model cards, risk registers, approval forms.

These artifacts matter, but they are not governance. Governance exists only where decisions can be influenced, constrained, or reversed.

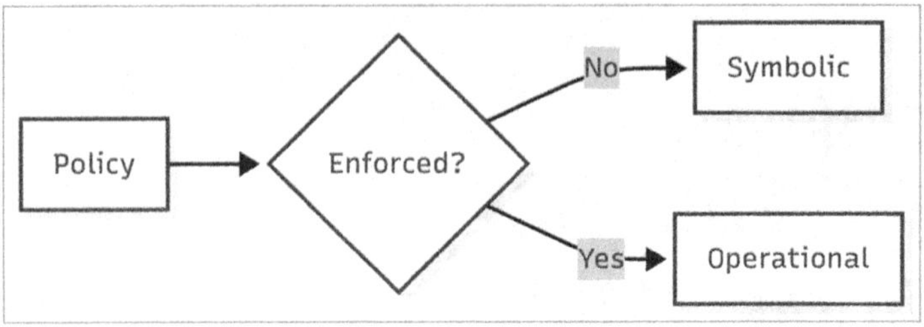

Figure 6.1 - Governance without enforcement is theater.

If a policy cannot change system behavior, it is informational at best.

EMBEDDING GOVERNANCE AT CONTROL POINTS

Effective governance operates at control points already established earlier:

- Legitimacy gates
- Feasibility assessments
- Design constraints
- Continuation decisions

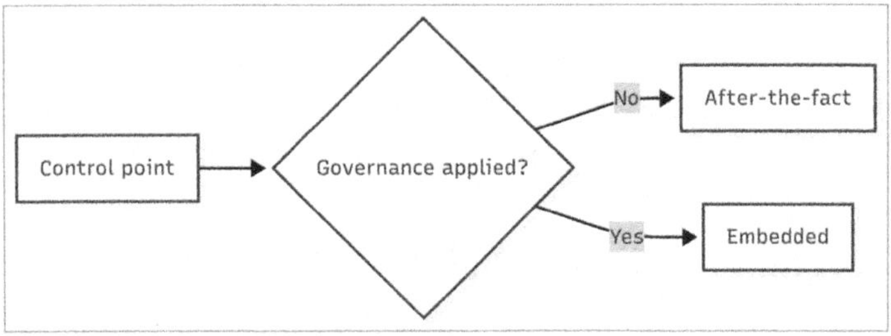

Figure 6.2 - Governance is most effective when it constrains real decisions.

Governance is most effective when it constrains real decisions.

COMPLIANCE AS AN OPERATING CONDITION

Compliance is often framed as a checklist. In practice, it is an ongoing operating condition.

Compliance feasibility depends on:

- Traceability of inputs and outputs
- Ability to reconstruct decisions
- Stability of documented behavior over time

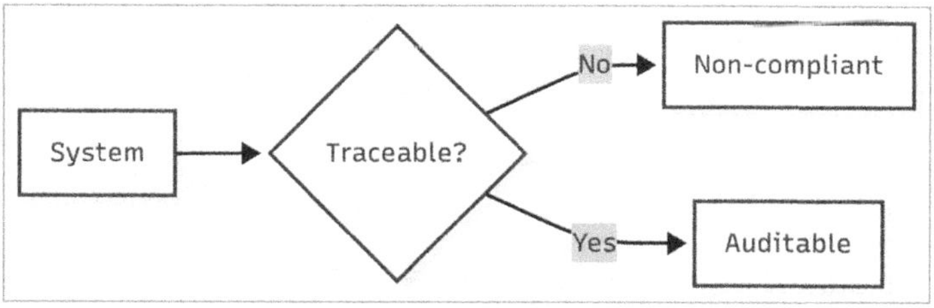

Figure 6.3 - If behavior cannot be reconstructed, it cannot be defended.

If behavior cannot be reconstructed, it cannot be defended.

ETHICS EMERGES FROM DEFAULTS

Ethics is rarely decided explicitly. It emerges from defaults.

Defaults determine:

- Who is affected automatically
- When humans are consulted
- How uncertainty is handled
- Which errors are invisible

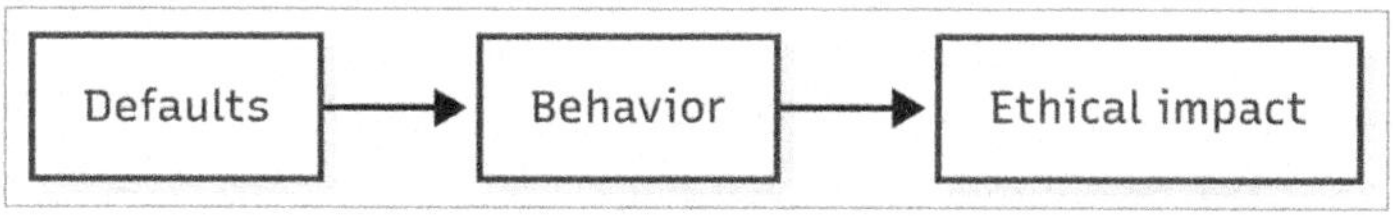

Figure 6.4 - Ethical outcomes are encoded long before ethical review.

Ethical review that ignores system defaults is necessarily incomplete.

ACCOUNTABILITY WITHOUT DIFFUSION

Governance fails when accountability is diffused.

Common failure modes include:

- Committees without decision rights
- Shared responsibility without ownership
- Escalation paths that never escalate

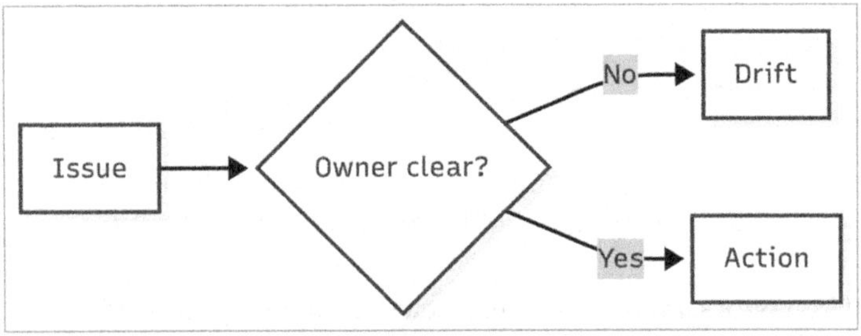

Figure 6.5 - Accountability must be singular to be effective.

Multiple reviewers do not create accountability; they obscure it.

RESPONDING TO INCIDENTS AND HARM

No governance framework prevents all harm. What matters is response.

An effective response requires:

- Predefined incident thresholds
- Authority to pause or roll back systems
- Clear communication channels

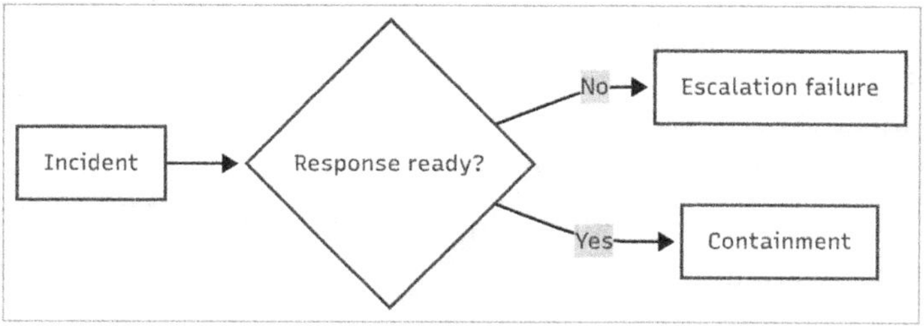

Figure 6.6 - Governance is tested under stress, not in steady state.

Delayed or ambiguous responses compound harm.

ETHICS COMMITTEES AND REALITY

Ethics committees can provide oversight, but they cannot substitute for operational design.

Their value depends on:

- Access to real system behavior
- Authority to stop or alter deployment
- Integration with engineering and product teams

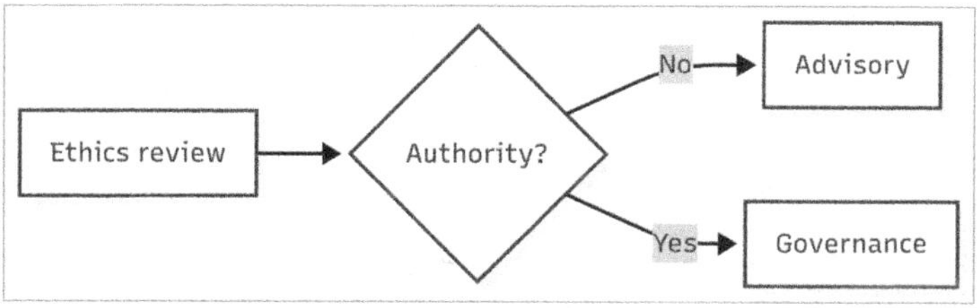

Figure 6.7 - Ethics without authority is commentary.

Without leverage, ethical guidance remains aspirational.

CLOSING

Governance, compliance, and ethics are not separate concerns layered onto AI systems. They are emergent properties of how systems are designed, integrated, measured, and maintained.

Treating them as operational disciplines, rather than moral overlays, does not weaken ethical responsibility. It is the only way to make it real.

The next chapter turns to **monitoring, drift, and accountability over time**, examining how systems change, and how responsibility persists, after deployment.

CHAPTER 7
MONITORING, DRIFT, AND ACCOUNTABILITY OVER TIME

Most AI systems do not fail at launch. They fail later, after approval, after integration, after initial success, when attention shifts and assumptions decay.

Time is the most underestimated risk factor in AI implementation. Models drift, data changes meaning, organizations evolve, and incentives shift. Accountability, however, rarely updates at the same pace.

This chapter focuses on what it takes to remain responsible *after* deployment, when systems are no longer novel but still consequential.

MONITORING IS A GOVERNANCE FUNCTION

Monitoring is often framed as a technical activity: tracking accuracy, latency, or uptime. In practice, monitoring is a governance function. It determines what the organization notices, and what it ignores.

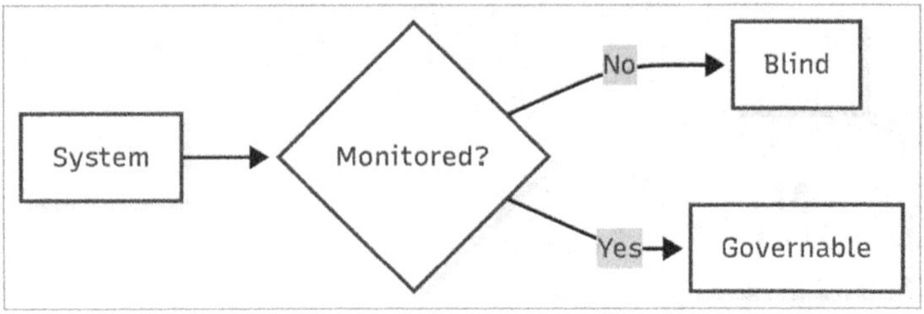

Figure 7.1 - What is not monitored cannot be governed.

If a system's behavior is not observable, accountability becomes hypothetical.

TECHNICAL DRIFT AND INSTITUTIONAL DRIFT

Drift is not singular.

- **Technical drift** occurs when data distributions, environments, or usage patterns change.
- **Institutional drift** occurs when goals, incentives, or oversight weaken over time.

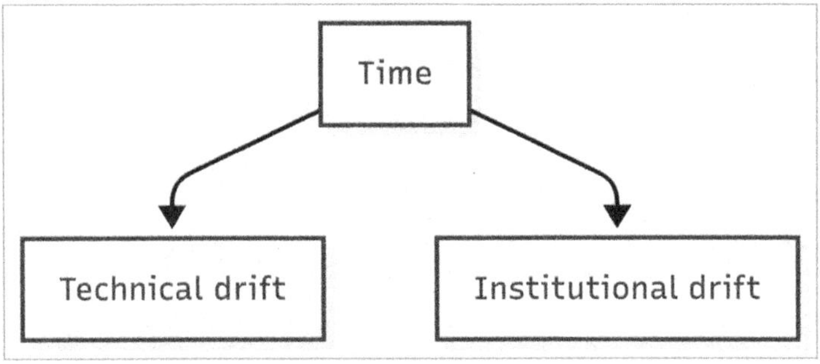

Figure 7.2 - Technical and institutional drift compound each other.

Most failures occur when both drift simultaneously and unnoticed.

SIGNALS WORTH MONITORING

Not all signals matter equally. Monitoring everything produces noise; monitoring the wrong things produces false confidence.

High-value signals typically include:

- Input distribution changes
- Override and escalation frequency
- Decision latency and bottlenecks
- Incident and near-miss reports

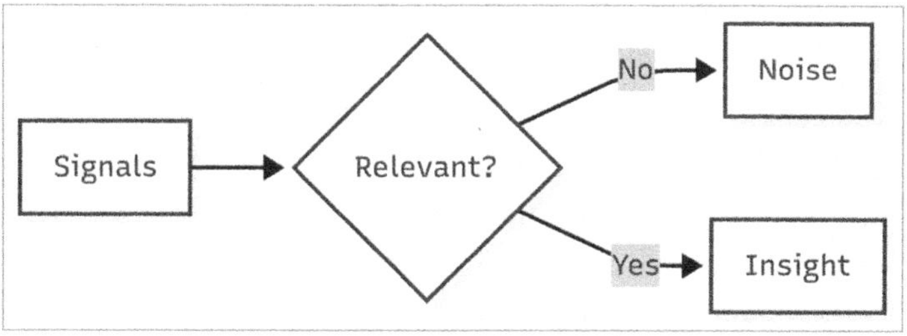

Figure 7.3 - Monitoring must privilege relevance over volume.

Choose signals that surface risk early, not those that confirm past success.

REVIEW CADENCE AND AUTHORITY

Monitoring without review is surveillance. Review without authority is ritual.

Effective accountability requires:

- Defined review intervals
- Clear decision rights at review points
- Authority to change, pause, or stop systems

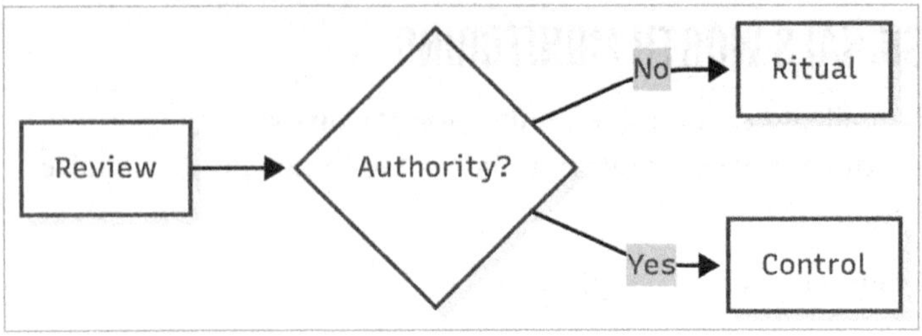

Figure 7.4 - Review only matters when it can change outcomes.

If no one can act on findings, monitoring serves no purpose.

Updating Models and Assumptions

Model updates are often treated as maintenance. In reality, they are scope changes.

Updates may:

- Alter error distributions
- Change who is affected
- Invalidate prior approvals

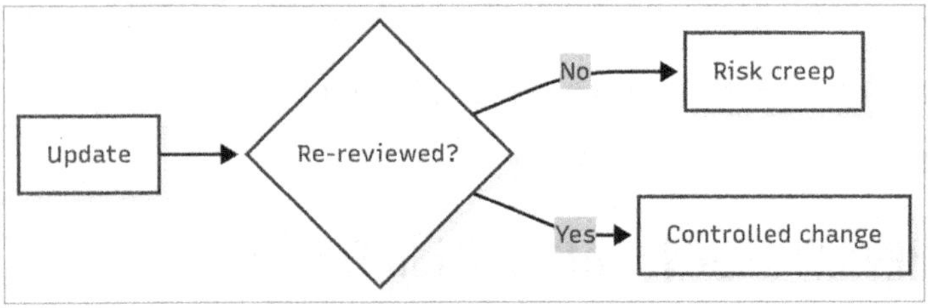

Figure 7.5 - Unreviewed updates accumulate hidden risk.

Every update should trigger proportional review, not automatic acceptance.

ACCOUNTABILITY OVER TIME

Accountability often erodes as systems age.

Common erosion patterns include:

- Original owners moving on
- Responsibility diffusing across teams
- Systems becoming "infrastructure" by default

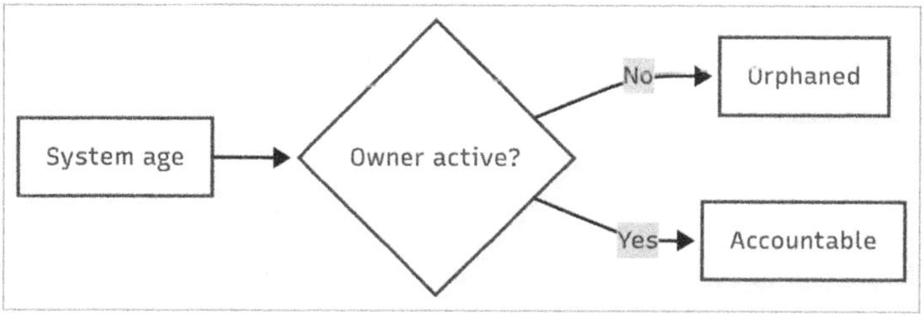

Figure 7.6 - Orphaned systems are governance failures waiting to surface.

Accountability must be renewed, not assumed.

PREPARING FOR FAILURE

Failure is not hypothetical. Responsible systems assume it.

Preparation includes:

- Incident playbooks
- Clear communication protocols
- Authority to suspend operation

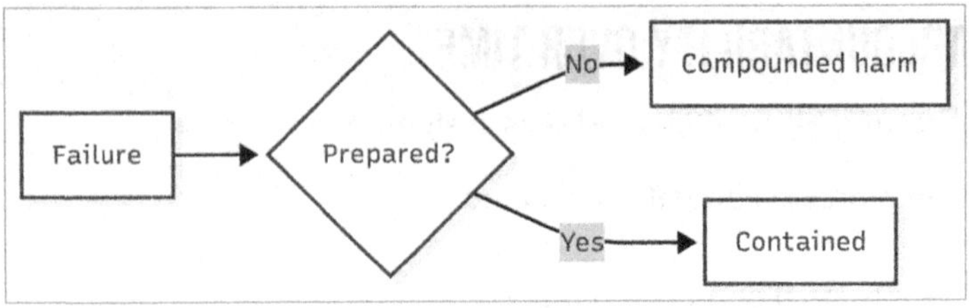

Figure 7.7 - Preparedness limits harm; improvisation amplifies it.

Organizations that rely on improvisation during failure tend to repeat it.

CLOSING

Accountability does not end at deployment. It intensifies.

Monitoring, review, and renewal are what prevent AI systems from becoming invisible liabilities. Responsibility over time is not a technical challenge, it is an institutional one.

The next chapter turns to **sunsetting, decommissioning, and organizational memory**, examining how systems end, and what remains after they do.

CHAPTER 8
SUNSETTING, DECOMMISSIONING, AND ORGANIZATIONAL MEMORY

Every AI system ends. Some are retired deliberately; others decay quietly until they are replaced, ignored, or become liabilities.

Sunsetting is rarely treated as part of implementation. As a result, organizations accumulate systems that no longer deliver value, can no longer be defended, and are no longer clearly owned.

This final chapter treats *ending* as a first-class responsibility. How systems are decommissioned, and what an organization learns from them, determines whether AI maturity compounds or resets with each cycle.

SUNSETTING IS NOT FAILURE

Stopping a system is often interpreted as evidence that it failed. Economically and ethically, the opposite is frequently true.

Sunsetting is appropriate when:

- Value has declined or plateaued
- Risk has increased beyond tolerance
- Context has changed such that prior legitimacy no longer holds

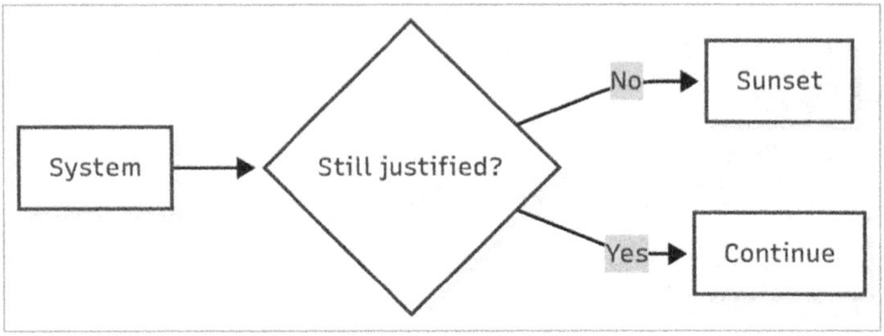

Figure 8.1 - Continuing is a decision; stopping is discipline.

Organizations that cannot stop systems do not govern them.

EXIT CRITERIA DEFINED UP FRONT

Responsible systems are built with exits in mind.

Exit criteria should be defined during framing and revisited during operation. Typical criteria include:

- Sustained negative ROI
- Repeated incidents or near-misses
- Loss of data legitimacy or consent
- Regulatory or policy change

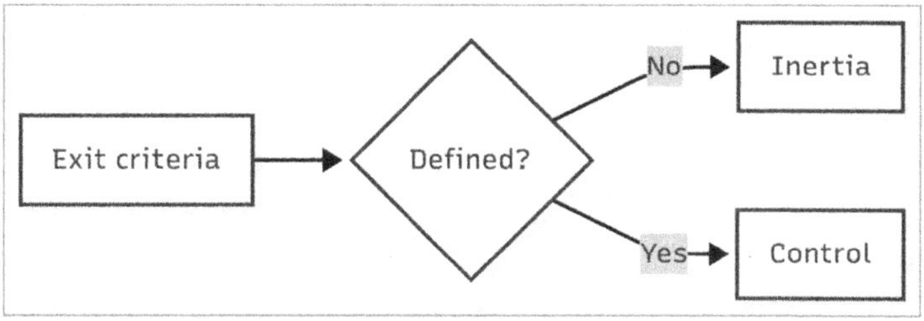

Figure 8.2 - Undefined exits guarantee prolonged risk.

Without explicit criteria, systems persist by default.

DECOMMISSIONING AS A PROCESS

Decommissioning is not a single action. It is a process that must be planned and executed deliberately.

Key elements include:

- Controlled shutdown or rollback
- Communication with affected users
- Transition of responsibilities
- Validation that dependencies are removed

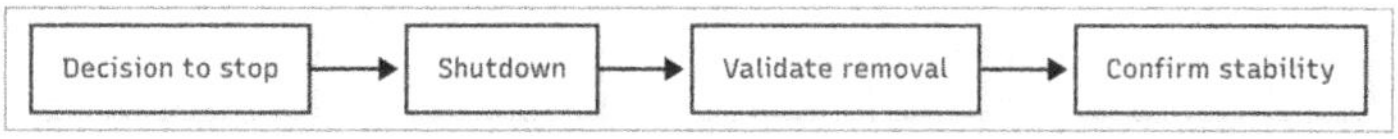

Figure 8.3 - Decommissioning failures often surface indirectly.

Abrupt or opaque shutdowns create new risks rather than resolving old ones.

DATA, MODELS, AND THE AFTERLIFE

Even after a system stops running, its artifacts remain.

Organizations must decide:

- What happens to retained data
- Whether trained models are archived, reused, or destroyed
- How consent and retention obligations are honored

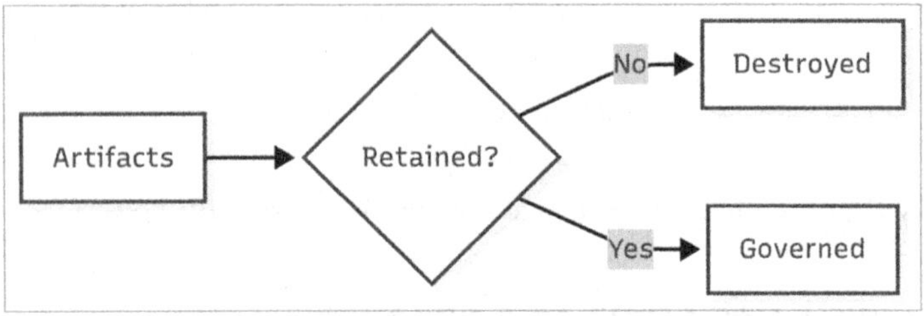

Figure 8.4 - Decommissioning includes data and models, not just code.

Unmanaged artifacts become compliance and reputational risks.

RESPONSIBILITY AFTER SHUTDOWN

Accountability does not end when a system stops operating.

Post-shutdown responsibilities may include:

- Responding to delayed harms
- Supporting audits or investigations
- Explaining past decisions

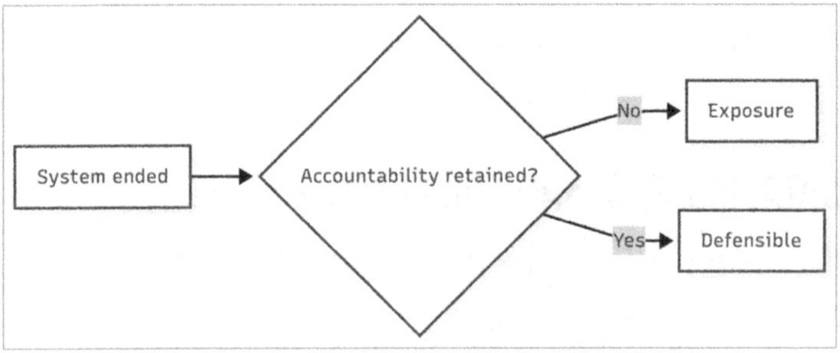

Figure 8.5 - Systems can outlive their operational footprint.

If no one remains accountable, responsibility has already failed.

ORGANIZATIONAL MEMORY

Most organizations repeat mistakes not because they are careless, but because they forget.

Sunsetting should produce durable artifacts:

- What problem was attempted
- What worked and what failed
- Which assumptions proved false
- What signals were missed

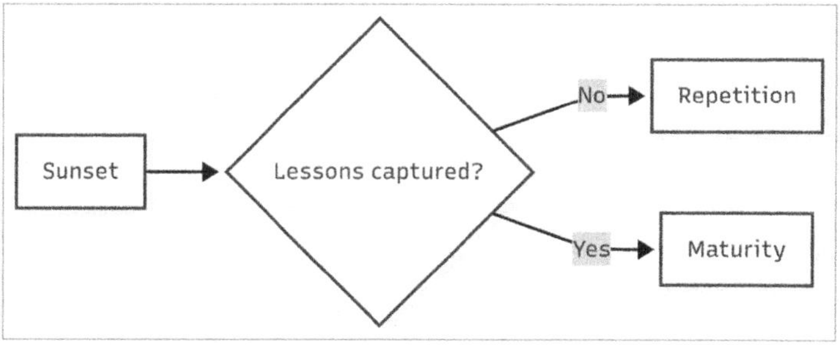

Figure 8.6 - Organizational memory determines whether experience compounds.

Without deliberate capture, learning is lost with staff turnover.

ENDING WELL

How a system ends shapes institutional trust.

Transparent sunsetting:

- Signals responsibility rather than failure
- Preserves credibility with users and regulators

- Makes future deployments easier to justify

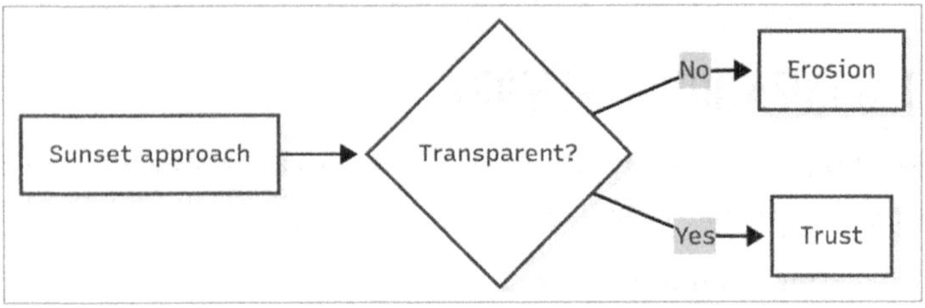

Figure 8.7 - Ending well is part of governing well.

Organizations that end systems cleanly are taken more seriously when they propose new ones.

CLOSING

This handbook began with a simple question: *should this system exist?* It ends with its counterpart: *when should it stop?*

Between those questions lies the full responsibility of AI implementation.

AI maturity is not measured by how many systems are deployed, but by how many are governed, maintained, and, when the time comes, retired deliberately.

The work of responsible implementation is cyclical. What you learn from one system is the legitimacy of the next.

APPENDIX

TERMS AS USED IN THIS BOOK

This appendix clarifies how certain terms are used *operationally* in this handbook. These are not general or industry-standard definitions. They are working meanings intended to support decision-making in real organizational contexts.

Feasibility

Feasibility means the ability of an organization to build, operate, govern, and sustain a system over time. It includes data rights, operational capacity, legal exposure, and institutional readiness. Technical possibility alone does not establish feasibility.

Governance

Governance refers to the mechanisms by which decisions about an AI system are made, reviewed, and enforced over time. It is not synonymous with policy documents, principles, or oversight committees. Governance exists only where authority, escalation paths, and intervention rights are explicit.

Intervention

Intervention is the practical ability to modify, pause, constrain, or stop a system once it is in use. A system that cannot be intervened upon in practice is considered fragile and ungovernable, regardless of intent or design.

Legitimacy

Legitimacy refers to whether an AI system is justified in existing at all within a given organizational, legal, and social context. It is not moral approval or executive sponsorship. A system is legitimate only if its purpose, scope, and potential harms can be reasonably defended *before* design or deployment.

Operational integration

Operational integration describes how a system fits into real workflows, incentives, and decision-making processes. Successful integration requires clarity of authority, appropriate trust calibration, and the ability to respond to failure. Deployment alone does not constitute integration.

Responsibility

Responsibility is accountability for outcomes, not participation in delivery. In this book, responsibility implies the authority to make decisions, intervene in operation, and recommend stopping a system. Shared effort without clear accountability does not constitute responsibility.

Risk Acceptance

Risk acceptance is an explicit decision to proceed despite known uncertainties or potential harms. In this book, risk is not considered accepted unless it is named, scoped, and owned by an accountable role. Implicit or assumed acceptance is treated as a governance failure.

Sunsetting

Sunsetting is the planned, governed retirement of an AI system. It is treated as a normal and responsible phase of the system lifecycle, not as an admission of failure. Systems that cannot be safely sunset represent ongoing risk.

Trust

Trust denotes the willingness of individuals or institutions to rely on a system in situations that carry risk. It is relational and contextual, not a property of a model. In this book, loss of trust is treated as an operational and institutional failure, not merely a perception problem.

Value

Value refers to realized benefit observed in practice, not anticipated benefit or theoretical capability. In this book, claims of value must be supported by evidence over time and weighed against accumulated cost and risk.

These definitions apply only within the scope of this handbook and are intended to support clarity, not standardization.

AFTERWORD

RESPONSIBILITY, REVISITED

This book was written for people who build AI systems in the space between ambition and constraint.

If you have read this far, you are likely responsible for systems that affect real decisions, real people, and real institutions, often without having full authority over the conditions in which those systems operate. You have likely felt pressure to move faster than clarity allows, to promise more certainty than the system can deliver, or to treat unresolved risk as a future problem.

The chapters you have just read are not a methodology. They are an orientation.

They argue for a simple but demanding idea: **responsibility in AI implementation is not a moment, a document, or a role. It is a practice sustained over time.**

RESPONSIBILITY IS SEQUENTIAL

One of the quiet failures of AI discourse is the belief that responsibility can be addressed all at once, through a framework, a committee, or a set of principles.

In practice, responsibility unfolds sequentially:

- first in deciding *whether* a system should exist,
- then in determining *whether it can be defended,*
- then in how it is designed, integrated, and funded,
- then in how it is governed, monitored, and eventually ended.

Skipping steps does not eliminate responsibility. It merely defers it, often to people who are least equipped to bear it.

RESPONSIBILITY IS NOT NEUTRAL

Every AI system redistributes agency.

It changes who decides, who notices, who is asked to intervene, and who is blamed when outcomes disappoint. These redistributions are not neutral side effects of technology; they are consequences of choices, some explicit, many implicit.

Taking responsibility does not mean avoiding these choices. It means making them *legible*, *defensible*, and *revisable*.

RESPONSIBILITY REQUIRES SAYING NO

One of the most under-appreciated skills in AI practice is the ability to stop.

To stop a system before it is built. To stop it when it no longer delivers value. To stop it when its risks exceed what can be responsibly managed.

These decisions are rarely rewarded. They are often invisible. But they are the difference between governance and accumulation.

RESPONSIBILITY IS SHARED, BUT NOT DIFFUSE

Many failures in AI systems are attributed to "shared responsibility." In practice, this often means that no one can act decisively.

Responsible systems require shared participation, but **singular accountability**. Someone must be able to answer, to decide, and to intervene. Without that clarity, responsibility becomes rhetorical.

WHAT THIS BOOK ASKS OF YOU

This handbook does not ask you to be perfect, prescient, or risk-free.

It asks you to be explicit.

Explicit about why a system exists. Explicit about what it costs. Explicit about who is harmed when it fails. Explicit about who can stop it.

If you do that consistently, you will prevent more harm than any single model improvement ever could.

WHAT COMES NEXT

The work of responsible AI implementation is cyclical. Each system you build reshapes the conditions under which the next one is proposed.

If this book has done its job, it has given you language to slow momentum when it matters, structure to surface tradeoffs early, and confidence to treat restraint as a form of competence.

AI systems will continue to improve. Institutions will continue to lag. The space between them is where your work lives.

That work matters.

ABOUT THE AUTHOR

Dom is an author, software architect, and founder-engineer focused on the practical implementation of AI systems in real organizations.

His work sits at the intersection of technology, governance, and organizational decision-making. He has spent his career building and evaluating systems that must operate under real constraints: regulatory scrutiny, economic pressure, institutional inertia, and human judgment.

Rather than treating AI as a purely technical problem, Dom focuses on the conditions under which AI systems succeed or fail once deployed: how responsibility is allocated, how risk accumulates over time, and how design and integration choices shape outcomes long after launch.

He is the founder of *Hypermodern AI,* the author of *Hypermodern Theorem* and the editor of *The Journal of Applied AI,* along with related essays exploring applied systems thinking, institutional design, and the unintended consequences of automation. His writing emphasizes restraint, accountability, and decision-making under uncertainty.

Applied AI Handbook reflects this perspective. It is written for practitioners who are accountable for outcomes, not just delivery; and who must navigate the gap between what AI systems can do and what organizations can responsibly sustain.

x.com/djocubeit
linkedin.com/in/jocubeit
amazon.com/author/jocubeit

Made in the USA
Monee, IL
04 November 2026

67383024R00046